IMPROPER CROSS-STITCH

IMPROPER Cross-Stitch

35+ PROPERLY NAUGHTY PATTERNS

Haley Pierson-Cox

St. Martin's Griffin ⚞ New York

www.stmartins.com

Interior photographs courtesy of the author
Designed by Michelle McMillian

The Library of Congress Cataloging-in-Publication Data is available upon request.

ISBN 978-1-250-08898-7 (paper over board)
ISBN 978-1-250-18505-1 (ebook)

Our books may be purchased in bulk for promotional, educational, or business use.
Please contact your local bookseller or the Macmillan Corporate and Premium Sales
Department at 1-800-221-7945, extension 5442, or by email at
MacmillanSpecialMarkets@macmillan.com.

First Edition: August 2018

10   9   8   7   6   5   4   3   2   1

For my husband,
who never thinks
it's strange
that sometimes my job
is stitching swears.

Contents

Acknowledgments

Like most things worth doing in the world of DIY, this book came about as the result of a ton of good, creative fun, hard work, and lots of support and pompom waving from my A+ collection of family, friends, and crafty coconspirators (and one very cranky Simon cat).

So, first, I'd like to thank my husband, Jeremy Cox, whose curiosity, drive to keep making and keep learning, and absolute belief in the value of creative work is a constant source of inspiration.

I'd like to thank my family, and especially my parents, for their unflinching belief that I can and will do anything that I put my mind to, which has long served as the foundation on which I've built my creative career.

I'd also like to thank my friends (especially my BFF, Melanie Sanders), who cheerfully and relentlessly asked me for book-related progress updates every single time they saw me, even when I was a total stressball. My friends really are the best!

A special thank-you goes out to Becky Stern, who braved the horrors of metallic thread to stitch the "Not a Dirty Word" pattern, which is the only project in the book that I didn't stitch myself.

Thank-yous are also owed to my publisher and the production and marketing teams that worked to get this book into the hands of stitchers—particularly to Lizzie Poteet, who was this book's first editor, and whose sense of humor and love of cross-stitch is largely the reason that the book exists. Thanks, too, to the book's editor, Hannah Braaten, who "got" it immediately.

Finally, I'd to thank my sweet Pixel cat, who passed away from cancer while I was writing this book, for providing all of the snuggles and purrs a girl could ever ask for. I love you, Cat Alarm. Rest in peace.

Introduction

In all my years of crafting, I've learned many things, but this simple fact remains one of the most important: There is absolutely nothing in this world quite so satisfying as enshrining something deeply inappropriate within the delicate threads of a cross-stitch sampler. It's truly one of life's great delights!

Now, perhaps the very idea of cross-stitch conjures up images of saccharine verses displayed in quaint bedoilied hellscapes, and you're suddenly wondering what you're doing here. Don't worry. I can assure you this is not that kind of book. Despite what many a disgruntled historical romance heroine may have led you to believe, needlework doesn't have to be boring or torturous. (If it is, you're probably just stitching the wrong kinds of designs. Put down your needle and step away from the geese in bonnets!) Instead, I'd like to show you how needlework can be a relaxing, fun, and surprisingly badass way to spend your downtime.

In this book, I'll introduce you to the joys of stitching the naughty, the profane, the irreverent, and the just plain awesome. And it'll be really fun, I promise! First, we'll start with a basic lesson in cross-stitch technique, no previous experience required. Then, once you know your way around an embroidery hoop and a skein of floss, we'll move on to the designs—thirty-two in total, ranging from hip to nerdy to ironically domestic—where you can embrace your inner snark with gleeful abandon. Finally, once you're an old pro with the needle, we'll wrap things up with three complete alphabets and a chart-your-own how-to, which you can use to customize the patterns in the book or to create original designs of your own!

One of my favorite things about stitching for my own personal pleasure is that it's all about doing whatever the hell I want simply because I feel like doing it, and I'm so excited to be able share some of that crafty freedom with you! Maybe you feel like dropping an F-bomb in the middle of an intricately designed flower scene? Or waxing poetic about bespectacled beauties? Or maybe you've discovered that the wall above your desk is suffering from a distressing lack of sarcasm? Whatever the reason, I think you'll find that within the orderly grid of the humble cross-stitch lies endless opportunity for creativity and misbehavior!

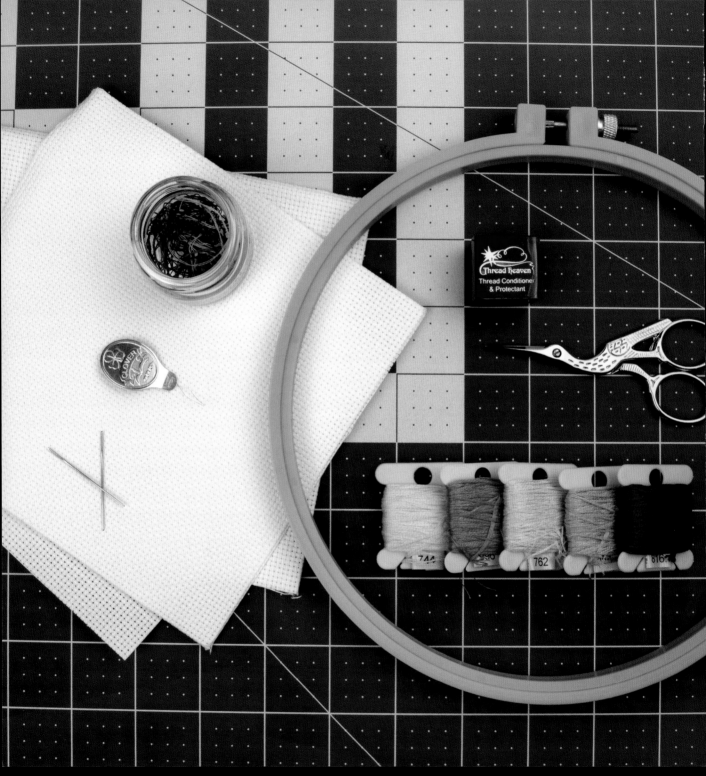

1. THE TOOLS OF THE CROSS-STITCH TRADE

Embroidery Floss

For the designs in this book, I used DMC cotton embroidery floss and DMC Light Effects metallic embroidery floss. In the color key included with each pattern, you'll find the DMC color codes for the specific colors that I used for the project.

When examining a skein of embroidery floss, you'll notice that each length can be separated into six individual strands of floss. (This is true for most brands of embroidery floss, not just DMC.) For the projects in this book, I used two or three strands at a time.

- -

Tip: Increasing the number of embroidery floss strands can make for a bolder, more textured look, but you should always add strands with caution—too many can make your project less crisp, make stitching harder, or even distort your fabric. Decreasing the number of strands can be helpful when stitching finer details.

- -

Tapestry Needles

Cross-stitch is generally worked with a tapestry needle, which has a blunt tip that slides easily through the holes in Aida cloth fabric and protects your fingers from unnecessary pokes. Tapestry needles also have a large eye that makes it easier to thread your needle with multiple strands of embroidery floss.

For size 14 Aida cloth (see the fabric section on page 4), you'll want to use a size 24 tapestry needle.

Choosing Your Fabric

Cross-stitch can be done on many different kinds of fabrics, but in this book we'll be using size 14 Aida cloth, which is a gridded cotton fabric made for cross-stitching that has fourteen squares per inch.

Why Aida cloth? Cross-stitch is easiest when it's done on an even-weave fabric that provides a nice square grid for the stitches. One of the most common fabrics used is Aida cloth, which is an open-weave, even-weave fabric, which means that, in addition to the fabric being woven in a way that creates a nice regular grid, small holes are also visible where the warp threads and weft threads cross (that's what makes it open weave). These tiny holes are perfect for stitching.

Aida cloth comes in many different sizes and colors. Beginning stitchers generally find it easier to work with larger grids, like the size 14 Aida cloth that we'll be using, and more advanced stitchers will enjoy the flexibility and room for detail afforded by smaller grid sizes. Similarly, beginners

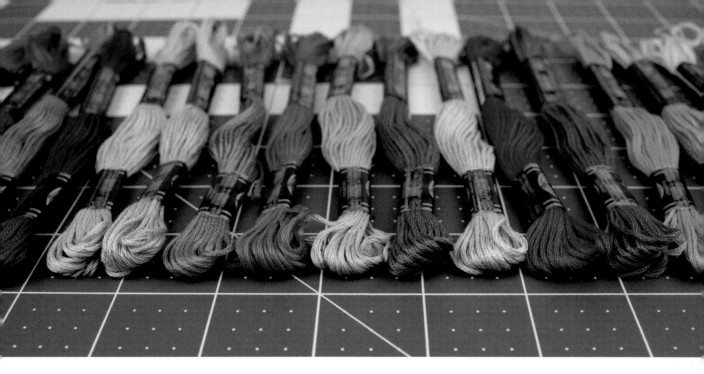

usually stick with white or natural colored fabric, on which the grid is easiest to see, but more advanced stitchers may want to branch out into brighter or darker colors.

EVEN WEAVE: The fabric has the same number of threads per inch both horizontally and vertically, creating a visible grid pattern (example: linen).

OPEN WEAVE: The fabric has intentional spaces between the threads in the weaving that create holes (example: Aida cloth).

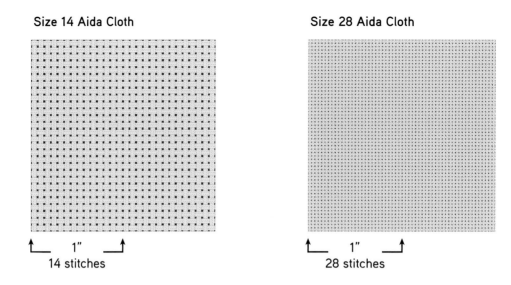

Size 14 Aida Cloth

Size 28 Aida Cloth

1"
14 stitches

1"
28 stitches

Fabrics like the Aida cloth that we'll be using are both even weave and open weave.

Introduction to Grid Size

For Aida cloth, the lower the size number, the larger the squares are in the grid.

As shown in the example above, a lower number like size 14 Aida cloth will have larger stitches—fourteen stitches per inch—and therefore a larger finished cross-stitched image than a project stitched on size 28 Aida cloth (twenty-eight stitches per inch).

Embroidery Hoops

Embroidery hoops hold fabric taut so it's easier to make smooth, even stitches with consistent floss tension.

There are a variety of different kinds of embroidery hoops available in craft stores, and a few of the most common options are wooden hoops, plastic hoops, plastic snap frames, and standing and seated hoops and frames.

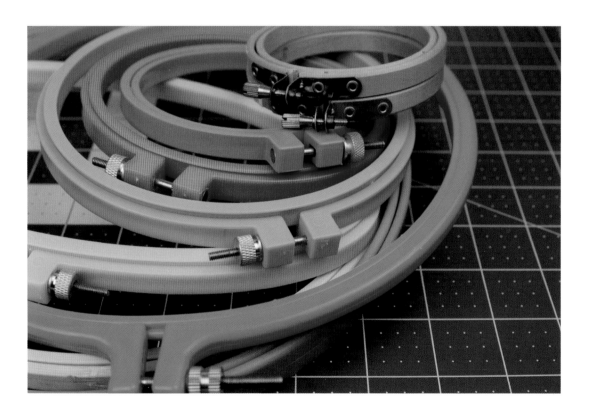

All of these hoops/frames are suitable for cross-stitch projects, so you should feel free to select the one that best suits your needs in a size (usually measured in diameter) that best fits your project.

I personally prefer a sturdy plastic frame when I'm stitching, so I used an 8-inch Susan Bates HOOP-La embroidery hoop for most of the projects in this book.

Additional Tools

In addition to the materials listed above, you'll also want to have the following items in your cross-stitch kit:

- A small pair of sharp embroidery scissors
- A needle threader (if needed)
- A little jar or plastic baggie to hold thread ends/scraps while you stitch (Fun fact: These little thread ends are affectionately called "orts" by many stitchers.)
- A thread conditioner (Optional, but highly recommended. I swear by Thread Heaven, which lessens the friction between the embroidery floss and the fabric, making it easier to stitch, then continues to protect your embroidery from stains and fading throughout the life of your project.)
- A fine-tip water-soluble fabric marker (Optional, but handy for adding an occasional mark or guide to your fabric that will wash away when your project is finished.)

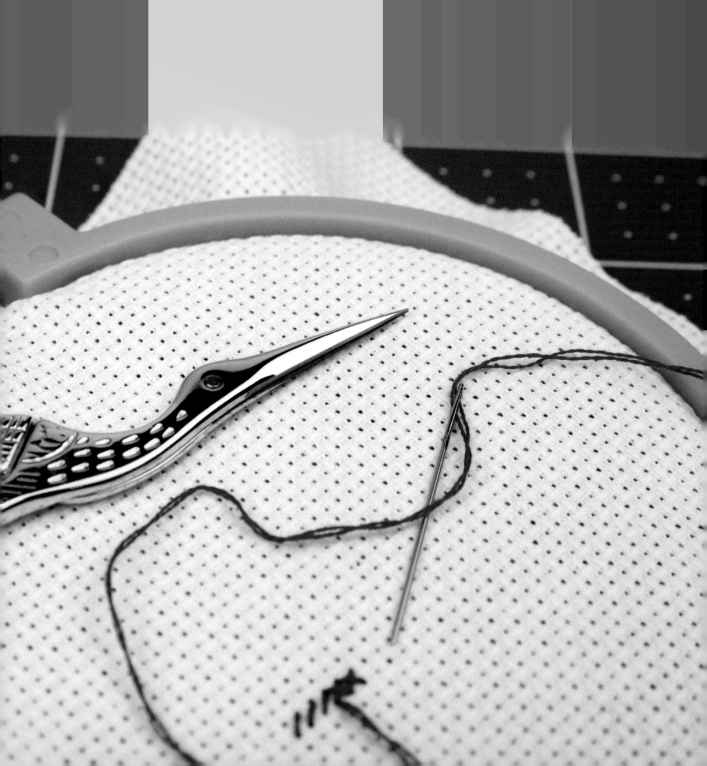

2. THE BASICS OF CROSS-STITCH

If anyone's feeling a touch of the I've-never-done-this-kind-of-craft-before jitters, let me set your mind at ease right away: While skilled stitchers certainly can and do create beautifully detailed and intricate cross-stitch designs, at its heart, cross-stitch is easy. When it comes right down to it, all you're really doing is putting an X in a box.

Cutting and Preparing Fabric

Cut a piece of fabric large enough to fit the whole pattern, plus an additional 4 inches on all sides. The extra inches will give you some room for error in case you miscount your stitches. They will also be helpful later when you're finishing and framing your project. Use fabric scissors or pinking shears (to avoid fraying) to make your cuts.

Tip: When I'm stitching on the go, I give my projects a little extra protection from fraying by using a liquid anti-fraying seam sealant like Fray Check along the edges.

Preparing Your Fabric and Pattern

Find and mark the center of your pattern lightly with a pencil (or, if you don't like to write in books, use a sticky note with an arrow drawn on it—that's what I do), then find and mark the center of your fabric with a water-soluble marker or fabric pencil.

Tip: Fold your fabric in half horizontally, then fold it in half again vertically and finger-press the folds. The point where the two temporary creases intersect is the center of your fabric.

Reading a Cross-Stitch Chart

A cross-stitch pattern is a grid, just like your cross-stitch fabric, and each square in the pattern grid corresponds to an individual square on your fabric.

Cross-stitch projects are worked across horizontal rows, and cross-stitch patterns are read the same way—generally from left to right. To begin, select a color, then work across the row, making stitches in the same places on the fabric that they appear on the pattern grid. Counting stitches across a grid might seem a bit tiresome at first, but it won't take long for the repetition to become both automatic and relaxing!

To avoid confusion, many people find it easiest to start stitching a design at the center row—where you've already marked both your fabric and your pattern—and work from there. This can help to ensure that the finished project is centered on the fabric and that you won't run out of room while stitching.

But if the idea of starting a pattern in the middle instead of at the beginning makes your skin crawl (raising my own hand, here), you can also use the grids on your fabric and on your pattern to count out the location of the first stitch in the first row of the pattern, using the center you marked on each as a common reference point. This method requires a bit more work, but it will have the anal among us sighing with relief.

Important: When working on a project, keep in mind that any outlines, French knots, or other decorative stitches should be done last. Complete all of the cross-stitches in the pattern first, then go back and add outlines or decorative stitches at the end.

How to Make a Cross-Stitch

A single cross-stitch consists of two diagonal stitches that cross in the center. To make the first stitch, insert the needle into the fabric from back

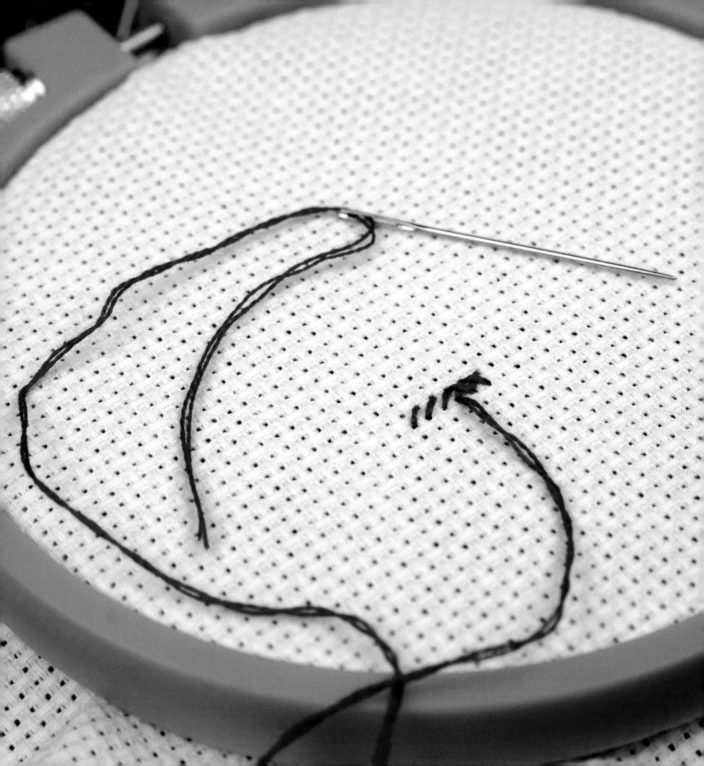

to front at point A and stitch into the fabric from front to back at point B. Repeat the process for the second stitch, starting at point C and stitching into point D.

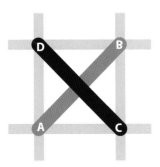

How to Work Multiple Cross-Stitches in a Row

When working a row with multiple cross-stitches in the same color, work all of the right-slanted stitches across the row first, then work back across the row in the opposite direction, completing the left-slanting stitches.

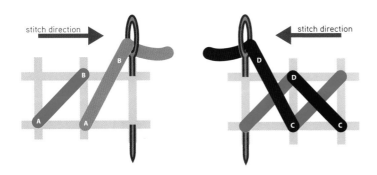

When working a row with more than one color, complete all the stitches in one color before moving on to the next color.

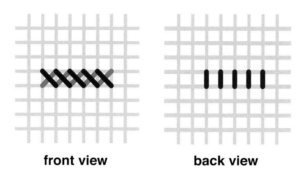

front view   **back view**

Tip: Some left-handed stitchers and/or stitchers who like to work out from the center of a pattern in both directions may find it more comfortable to work their cross-stitch rows from right to left. To give it a try, reverse the direction of the cross-stitch by stitching from B to A, then crossing the stitch from D to C.

Wondering why my reversed stitches start at B instead of C? Aesthetics is the answer! If you happen to be working the pattern from the center out, or if you decide to change stitching directions in the middle of a project, starting the reversed stitch at B will ensure that all of your finished stitches cross in the same direction (that means that the top stitches of each cross-stitch all slant diagonally in the same direction), whether you're stitching from right to left, left to right, or any combination of the two. Because while it might not seem important when you're working on an individual stitch, this kind of inconsistency is really noticeable and distracting in a finished project.

Bottom line: If you learned a different cross-stitch method from your favorite aunt, or if you simply find that making your stitches in a different way than I do feels more natural, knock yourself out! In the end, as long as all of your stitches cross in the same direction, it doesn't really matter how you start your stitch.

_ _

No Knots: Starting and Finishing Cross-Stitch Projects

Instead of knotting off the floss at the beginning/end of your project or when you run out of floss, which can cause unwanted bumps on the back that might be visible in your finished items, use your stitches to secure your floss ends in place.

Here's how it's done:

Starting a New Length of Floss or a New Color

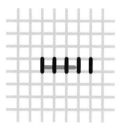

When starting a new length of floss or a new color, leave a tail about 2 inches long on the back of the project, then carefully stitch over the tail with your first few stitches to secure it in place. Use scissors to trim any extra length once the tail has been secured.

Finishing a Length of Floss or a Color

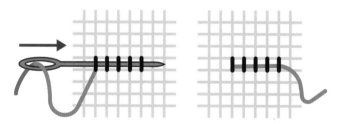

When you have about 3 inches left in a length of floss or when you reach the end of a color, slip the needle under several stitches on the back of your project, then pull the end of the floss through. Trim any extra length with a pair of scissors.

Tip: When cutting embroidery floss for your project, use your arm—shoulder to fingertips—as a length guide. Resist the urge to save time by cutting longer pieces; sections of floss that are too long are more likely to knot and tangle while you're stitching.

Additional Decorative Stitches: Backstitch

Backstitch is a versatile embroidery stitch that produces a neat, unbroken line of straight stitches. It's often used to outline shapes in cross-stitch projects. It's also great for adding decorative details like facial expressions, borders, or contrasting highlights to more complex designs, and it's a go-to stitch for simple lettering.

In the instructions below, the stitch is worked in a backward line (right to left, or counterclockwise, in the case of outlines).

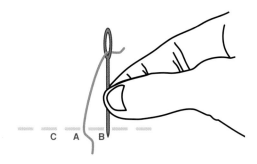

To start, insert your needle into the fabric from back to front at point A, then stitch forward from front to back at point B.

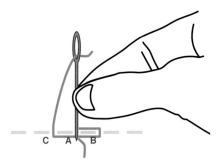

To make the second stitch in the line, insert your needle into the fabric from back to front at point C, then stitch backward into the end of your first stitch at point A.

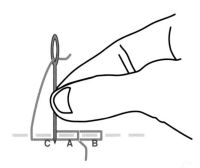

Continue the line by inserting the needle from back to front in the next open hole in the grid, then stitching backward into the end of the previous stitch.

Additional Decorative Stitches: French Knot

Now we come to the often-dreaded but undeniably pretty French knot.

It has a bit of a reputation for being a difficult and fussy stitch, but that's mostly just nonsense. It may take you a few tries to get the hang of it—it's an entirely different kind of stitch from those we've been making thus far, after all—but it's not actually very hard to do.

For this stitch, it's okay if you're not stitching directly into the holes in the grid. In fact, I usually position my French knots right in the center of a square so the solid fabric can help keep them in position.

Insert the needle into the fabric from back to front at point A, then rest your embroidery hoop on your knees/worktable so both hands are free.

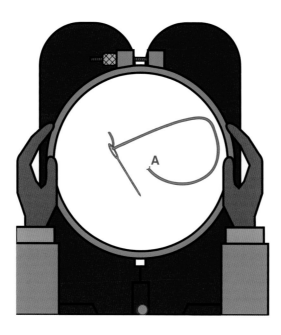

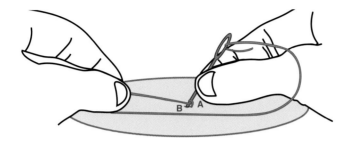

Gently pull the length of floss taut and position your needle an inch or so above the surface of the fabric. Use the hand that isn't holding your needle to wrap the floss around the end of the needle one to two times in a counterclockwise direction (once makes a smaller knot, twice makes a larger knot), taking care to maintain the gentle tension in the floss so the loops around the needle remain tight.

Still keeping those loops around the needle pulled tight with your non-needle hand, insert the tip of the needle into the fabric at point B, right

- -

Tip: The French knot is one of the few instances in cross-stitch where it's sometimes preferable to knot your floss end before starting the stitch to ensure that your floss remains securely in place while you work. My rule of thumb: If it's possible to secure your floss end under previous stitches before making your French knot, do that. But if your French knot is going to be placed in a location without many other stitches nearby to hold the floss in place, go ahead and make a knot if needed.

- -

next to point A. With the tip of the needle anchored in the fabric, use the hand holding the floss (still taut!) to pull the floss loops down the needle so they rest right against the fabric.

Carefully pick up your hoop and slowly pull the needle the rest of the way through the fabric from front to back to finish the stitch.

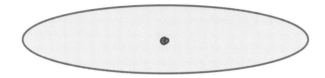

- -

Tip: Once the floss loops are resting against the fabric, I like to use the thumbnail on my non-needle hand to hold those loops in place while I finish the stitch. I think holding those loops in place gives me neater, more consistent results.

- -

Here's a handy stitch key that'll help you identify which stitches to use so you'll be reading the cross-stitch patterns in this book like a pro in no time. (The color key below each pattern is just a quick way to reference the colors used in each project.)

Stitch Key:

■	Cross-stitch
◣ or ◥	Half cross-stitch, slanted right
◤ or ◢	Half cross-stitch, slanted left
●	French knot
▬	Backstitch (lines and outlines)

3. HIPSTER SNARK

List of Patterns

- Cat Lady for Life
- Say It with Flowers
- Make It Modern
- Pup Rock
- Sweet Campfire Dreams
- Bike Date
- Nope
- Unexpected Tea Party
- Not a Dirty Word
- Zero Fucks Given

Hello! Welcome to the Hipster Snark pattern section. Grab a drink, scratch the cat behind the ears, and get ready to start a project that walks that fine line between super-cute and I-can't-believe-you-just-said-that.

Cat Lady for Life

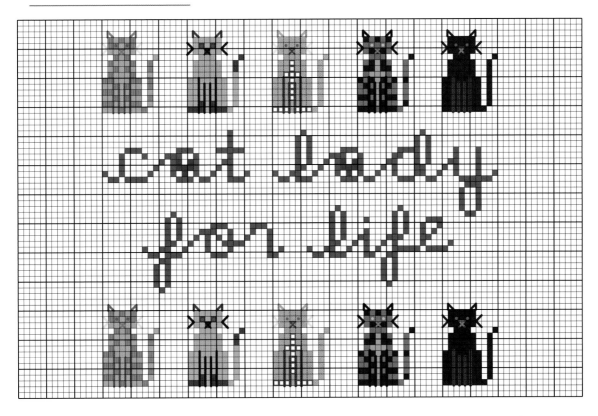

- ■ Black (DMC 310)
- ▨ Dark gray (DMC 414)
- ☐ White (DMC B5200)
- ■ Red (DMC 321)
- ■ Tan (DMC 3045)
- ▨ Beige (DMC 644)
- ■ Brown (DMC 838)
- ■ Light brown (DMC 3857)

- ■ Blue (DMC 796)
- ▨ Pumpkin orange (DMC 970)
- ▨ Light orange (DMC 3854)
- ▬ Pink (DMC 956)
- ▬ Brown (DMC 838)
- ▬ Light brown (DMC 3857)
- ▬ Pumpkin orange (DMC 970)
- ▬ Black (DMC 310)

- ▬ Charcoal gray (DMC 413)
- ▬ Dark gray (DMC 414)
- ▬ Light gray (DMC 415)
- ● Blue (DMC 796)
- ● Green (DMC 701)
- ● Chartreuse (DMC 906)

Say It with Flowers

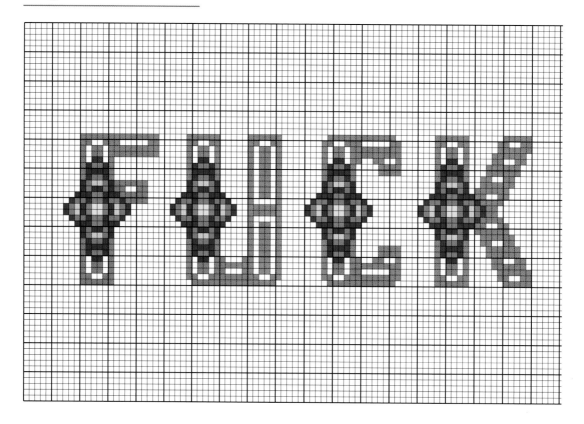

■ Dark gray (DMC 414)

■ Dark purple (DMC 333)

■ Medium purple (DMC 340)

□ Light purple (DMC 3747)

■ Dark green (DMC 319)

■ Green (DMC 701)

■ Gold (DMC 680)

□ Light yellow (DMC 744)

Making&
Music&
Books&
Art.

Make It Modern

- ■ Aqua (DMC 163)
- ■ Bright green (DMC 704)
- ■ Bright blue (DMC 3765)
- ■ Red orange (DMC 606)

Pup Rock

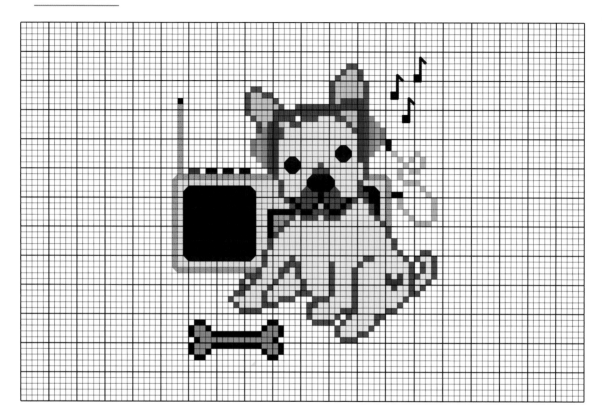

- ■ Soft black (DMC 3799)
- ■ Dark gray (DMC 414)
- ░ Light gray (DMC 415)
- ■ Medium brown (DMC 840)
- ░ Cream (DMC 739)
- ■ Light blue (DMC 3843)
- ■ Green (DMC 701)
- ■ Medium orange (DMC 741)
- ■ Dark purple (DMC 333)
- ■ Medium purple (DMC 340)
- ■ Red (DMC 321)
- ░ Light pink (DMC 3326)
- ▬ Soft black (DMC 3799)

Sweet Campfire Dreams

- ☐ White (DMC B5200)
- ░ Light gray (DMC 415)
- ▪ Dark gray (DMC 414)
- ▪ Red orange (DMC 606)
- ▪ Orange (DMC 740)
- ░ Dark yellow (DMC 972)
- ░ Very light yellow (DMC 727)
- ■ Chocolate brown (DMC 3882)
- ▪ Tan (DMC 3045)
- ■ Green (DMC 701)
- ▪ Bright green (DMC 704)
- ░ Sea green (DMC 164)
- ■ Soft black (DMC 3799)
- ░ Turquoise blue (DMC 3890)
- ▬ Soft black (DMC 3799)
- ▬ Dark gray (DMC 414)
- ▬ Turquoise blue (DMC 3890)
- ▬ Dark yellow (DMC 972)
- ▬ Red orange (DMC 606)
- ▬ Sea green (DMC 164)
- ▬ Tan (DMC 3045)
- ● Soft black (DMC 3799)

Bike Date

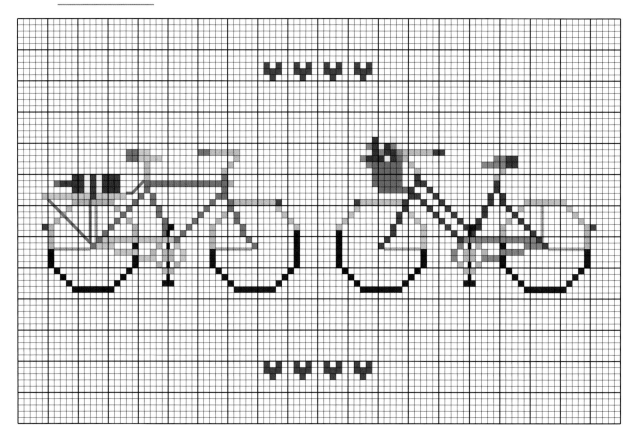

- ■ Soft black (DMC 3799)
- ■ Light gray (DMC 415)
- ■ Slate blue (DMC 3885)
- ■ Baby blue (DMC 827)
- ■ Red (DMC 321)
- ■ Forest green (DMC 986)
- ■ Grass green (DMC 989)
- ■ Dark yellow (DMC 972)
- ■ Very light yellow (DMC 727)
- ■ Chocolate brown (DMC 3882)
- ■ Tan (DMC 3045)
- ■ Dark purple (DMC 333)
- ■ Burgundy (DMC 917)
- ▬ Light gray (DMC 415)
- ▬ Soft black (DMC 3799)
- ▬ Slate blue (DMC 3885)

Nope

- ■ Dark pink (DMC 3804)
- Faded yellow (DMC 745)
- ■ Light violet (DMC 156)
- ▬ Medium purple (DMC 340)

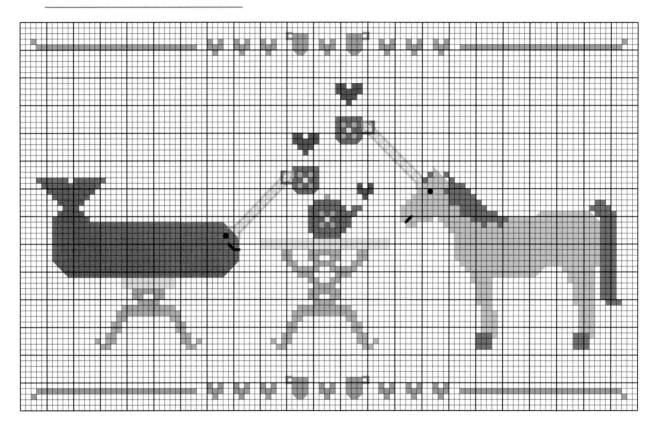

■ Gold (DMC 680)
■ Blue gray (DMC 798)
□ Baby blue (DMC 827)
■ Dark gray (DMC 414)
■ Slate gray (DMC 931)

□ Light gray (DMC 415)
□ Rose pink (DMC 605)
■ Bright red (DMC 349)
■ Dark purple (DMC 333)
□ Light yellow (DMC 744)

■ Soft green (DMC 3348)
— Black (DMC 310)
— Gold (DMC 680)
— Blue gray (DMC 798)
● Black (DMC 310)

Not a Dirty Word

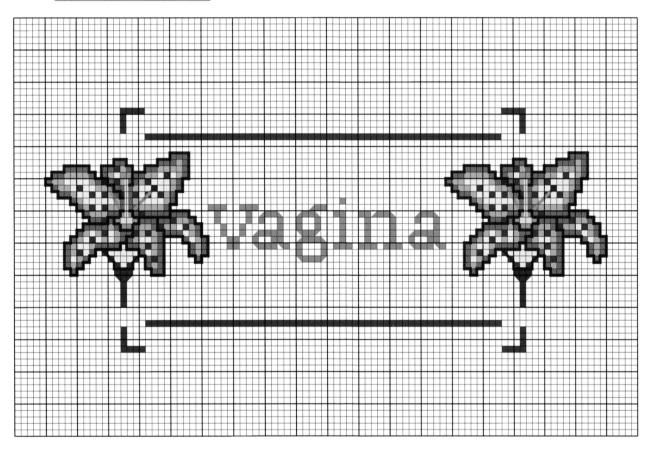

- Gold or metallic gold (DMC 680/E3852)
- Forest green (DMC 986)
- Dark red (DMC 498)
- Dark rose pink (DMC 602)
- Medium rose pink (DMC 603)
- Pale pink (DMC 151)
- Bright orange (DMC 742)
- Yellow (DMC 444)
- Coffee brown (DMC 938)
- Stone gray (DMC 317)
- Bright green (DMC 704)
- Yellow (DMC 444)

Zero Fucks Given

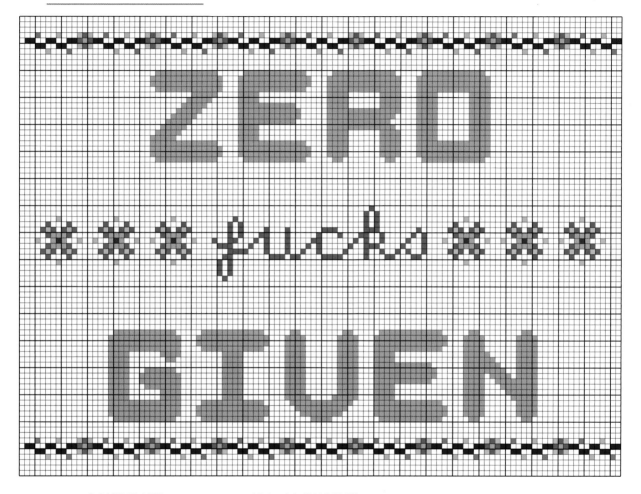

- ■ Gold (DMC 680)
- ■ Dark forest green (DMC 699)
- ■ Green (DMC 701)
- ■ Bright green (DMC 704)
- ■ Light pink (DMC 3326)
- ■ Dark pink (DMC 3804)
- ■ Burgundy (DMC 917)
- ■ Red orange (DMC 606)

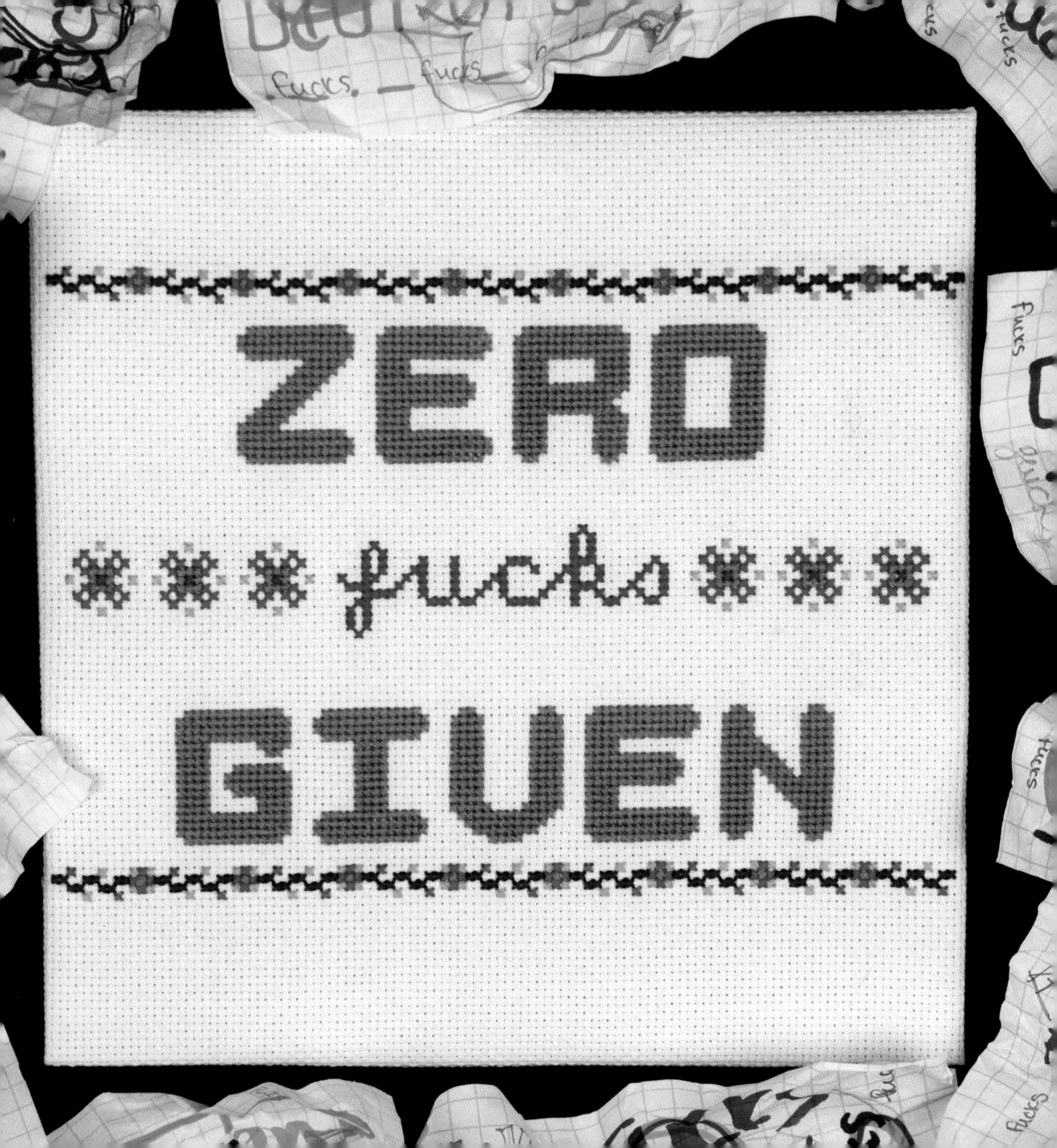
ZERO
fucks
GIVEN

4. IRONICALLY DOMESTIC

List of Patterns

- × Badass Garden Gnomes
- × Full Metal Feminist
- × 99 Problems
- × Home Is Where My Hound Is
- × Wine and Cats
- × I'll Cut You
- × Classic Libations
- × Armed and Creative
- × Home Sweet Castle
- × Stitchers Gonna Stitch
- × That Escalated Quickly
- × Damn, It Feels Good

Ever wondered what would happen if Morticia Addams were BFFs with Martha Stewart? Well, I'd like to think that it'd look a bit like the Ironically Domestic pattern section: Sugar and spice and "Wait. What the hell?"

Badass Garden Gnomes

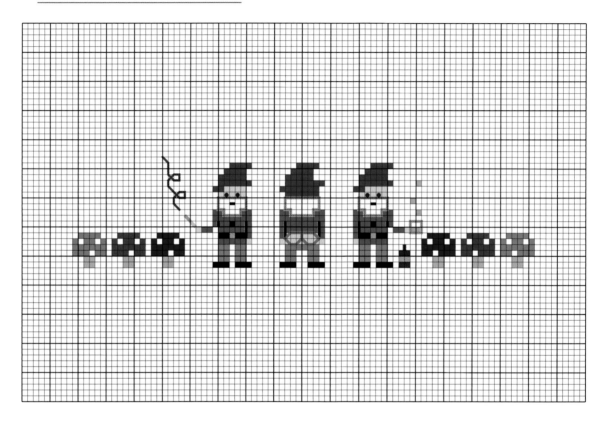

- ■ Medium blue (DMC 3891)
- ■ Light gray (DMC 415)
- □ White (DMC B5200)
- ■ Soft black (DMC 3799)
- ▪ Peach (DMC 3893)

- ▪ Beige (DMC 644)
- ■ Chocolate brown (DMC 3882)
- ▪ Dark yellow (DMC 972)
- ▪ Green (DMC 701)
- ■ Dark violet (DMC 3887)

- ■ Brick red (DMC 815)
- ▬ Soft black (DMC 3799)
- ▬ Light gray (DMC 415)
- ▬ Dark gray (DMC 414)
- ▬ Medium brown (DMC 840)
- ● Blue (DMC 796)

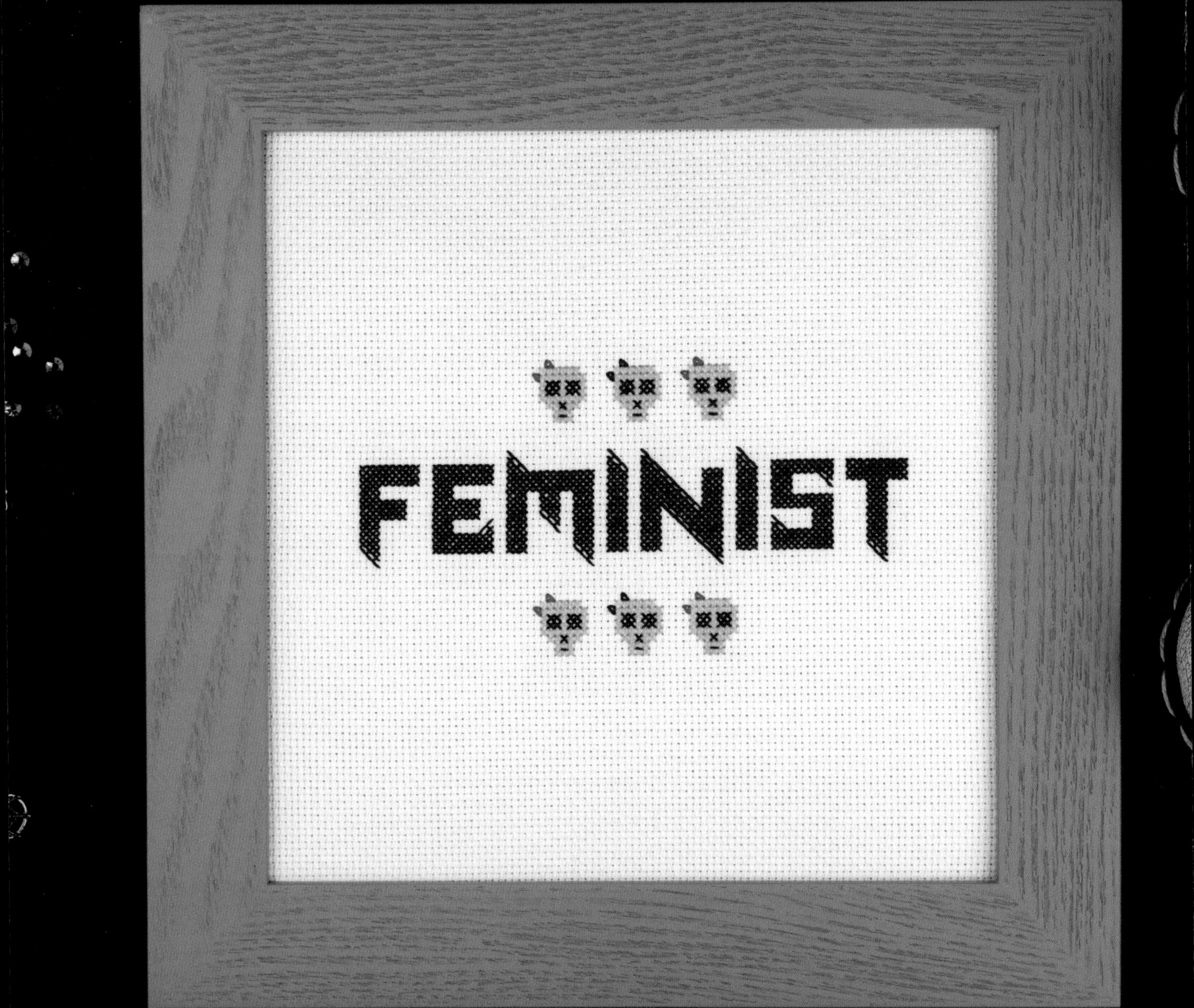
FEMINIST

Full Metal Feminist

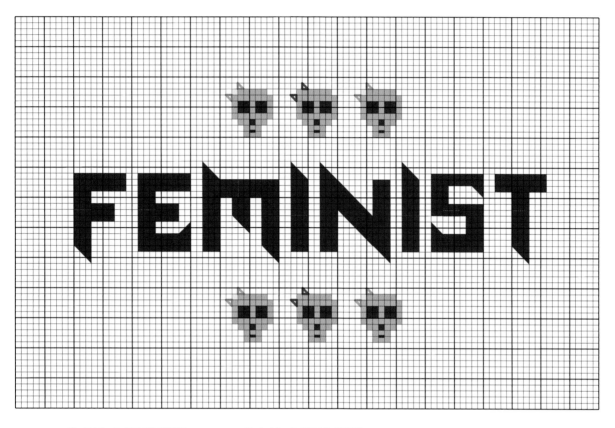

- ■ Soft black (DMC 3799)
- ■ Beige (DMC 644)
- ■ Pale pink (DMC 151)
- ■ Light purple (DMC 3747)

- ▬ Soft black (DMC 3799)
- ▬ Dark rose pink (DMC 602)
- ▬ Dark violet (DMC 3887)

- ■ Grass green (DMC 989)
- ■ Dark forest green (DMC 699)
- ■ Slate blue (DMC 3885)
- ■ Baby blue (DMC 827)
- ■ Light violet (DMC 156)
- ■ Light pink (DMC 3326)
- ■ Medium rose (DMC 603)
- ■ Bright yellow (DMC 726)
- ■ Dark gray (DMC 414)

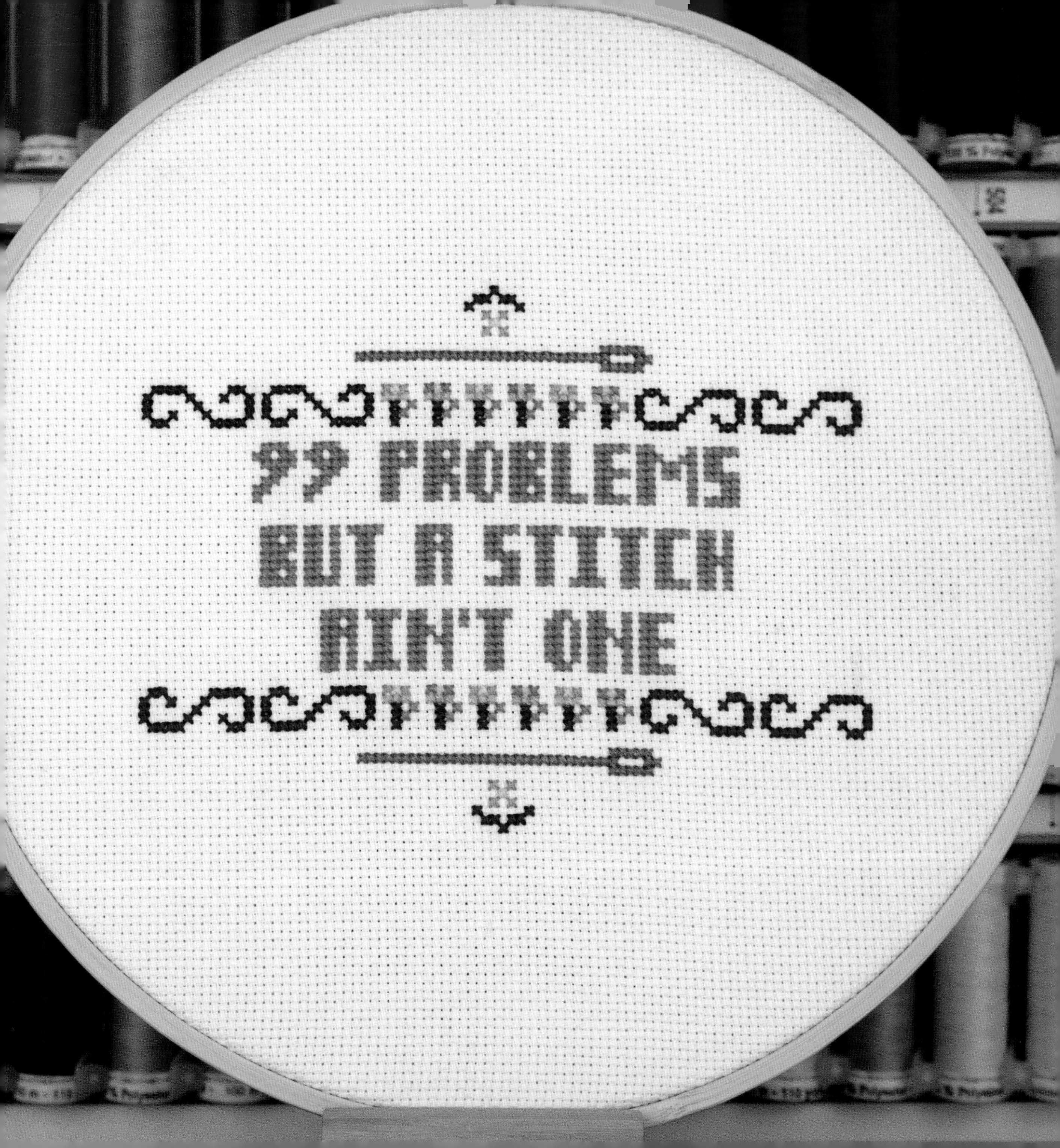
99 PROBLEMS
BUT A STITCH
AIN'T ONE

- ■ Black (DMC 310)
- ■ Soft black (DMC 3799)
- ▨ Light gray (DMC 415)
- ■ Brick red (DMC 815)
- ■ Forest green (DMC 986)
- ▨ Gold (DMC 680)
- ▨ Light yellow (DMC 744)
-   Beige (DMC 644)
- ■ Brown (DMC 838)
- ■ Medium brown (DMC 840)
- ▨ Salmon pink (DMC 3833)
- ▬ Black (DMC 310)
- ▬ Medium brown (DMC 840)
- ● Black (DMC 310)
- ● Light blue (DMC 3843)
- ● Brown (DMC 838)

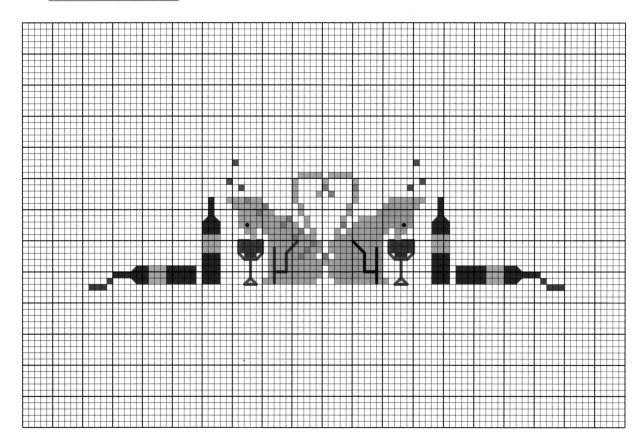

- ■ Light blue (DMC 3843)
- ■ Forest green (DMC 986)
- ■ Brick red (DMC 815)
- ▪ Light pink (DMC 3326)
- ▪ Burnt orange (DMC 946)
- ▪ Dark yellow (DMC 972)
- ▪ Beige (DMC 644)
- ▪ Light gray (DMC 415)
- ▬ Chocolate brown (DMC 3882)
- ▬ Black (DMC 310)
- ▬ Light blue (DMC 3843)
- ● Black (DMC 310)

I'll Cut You

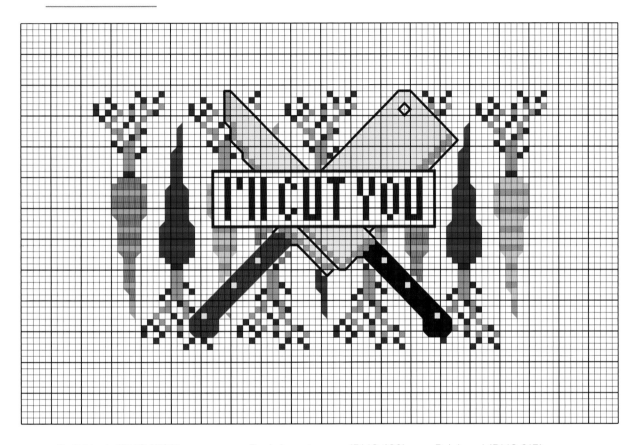

- ■ Soft black (DMC 3799)
- ■ Blue (DMC 796)
- ■ Dark gray (DMC 414)
- Light gray (DMC 415)
- ■ Chocolate brown (DMC 3882)
- ■ Dark forest green (DMC 699)
- ■ Grass green (DMC 989)
- ■ Orange (DMC 740)
- ■ Dark yellow (DMC 972)
- ■ Dark violet (DMC 3887)
- ■ Brick red (DMC 815)
- Very light yellow (DMC 727)
- ▬ Soft black (DMC 3799)
- ▬ Blue (DMC 796)

Classic Libations

- ■ Dark purple (DMC 333)
- ■ Light violet (DMC 156)
- ■ Brick red (DMC 815)
- ■ Light red (DMC 817)
- ■ Grass green (DMC 989)
- ■ Bright yellow (DMC 726)
- ■ Baby blue (DMC 827)
- ━ Chocolate brown (DMC 3882)
- ━ Brick red (DMC 815)
- ━ Light red (DMC 817)
- ━ Dark gray (DMC 414)

- ■ Charcoal gray (DMC 413)
- ■ Dark gray (DMC 414)
- □ Very light gray (DMC 762)
- ■ Blue (DMC 796)
- ■ Light blue (DMC 3843)
- ■ Red (DMC 321)

- ■ Salmon pink (DMC 3833)
- ■ Dark forest green (DMC 699)
- ■ Sea green (DMC 164)
- ■ Gold (DMC 680)
- ■ Burnt orange (DMC 946)
- ■ Dark yellow (DMC 972)

- ■ Bright yellow (DMC 726)
- □ Faded yellow (DMC 745)
- ■ Dark purple (DMC 333)
- ■ Soft purple (DMC 210)
- ▬ Charcoal gray (DMC 413)
- ▬ Very light gray (DMC 762)
- ▬ Sea green (DMC 164)

Home Sweet Castle

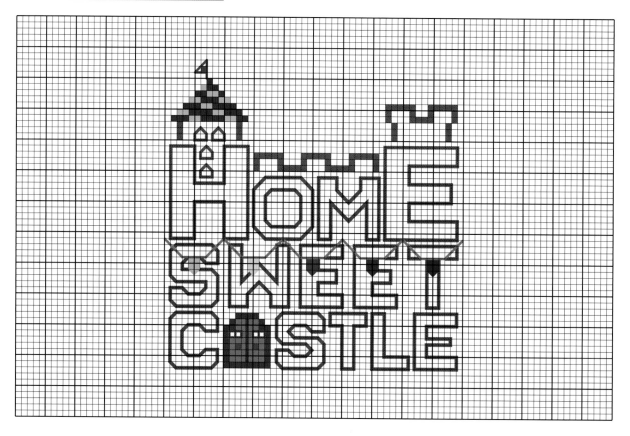

- ■ Soft black (DMC 3799)
- ■ Slate blue (DMC 3885)
- ▪ Sky blue (DMC 996)
- ■ Light red (DMC 817)
- ■ Brown (DMC 838)
- ▪ Tan (DMC 3045)
- ▫ Bright yellow (DMC 726)
- ■ Dark violet (DMC 3887)
- ▬ Brown (DMC 838)
- ▬ Tan (DMC 3045)
- ▬ Soft black (DMC 3799)
- ▬ Light red (DMC 817)

Stitchers Gonna Stitch

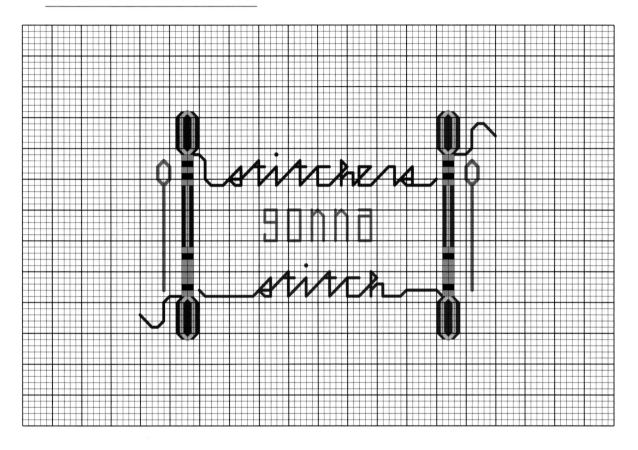

■ Soft black (DMC 3799)

■ Gold (DMC 680)

■ Blue (DMC 796)

■ Dark purple (DMC 333)

▬ Dark gray (DMC 414)

▬ Blue (DMC 796)

▬ Baby blue (DMC 827)

▬ Dark pink (DMC 3804)

▬ Dark purple (DMC 333)

▬ Soft purple (DMC 210)

● Blue (DMC 796)

● Dark purple (DMC 333)

That Escalated Quickly

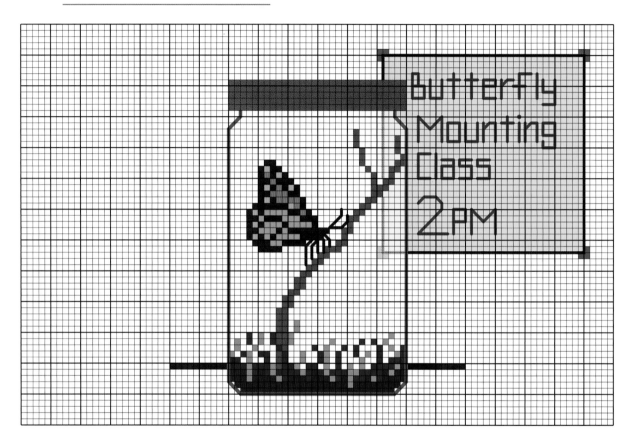

- ■ Soft black (DMC 3799)
- ■ Beige (DMC 644)
- ■ Brown (DMC 838)
- ■ Medium brown (DMC 840)
- ■ Dark forest green (DMC 699)
- ■ Grass green (DMC 989)

- ■ Red orange (DMC 606)
- ■ Medium orange (DMC 741)
- ■ Dark gray (DMC 414)
- ■ Slate blue (DMC 3885)
- ■ Light baby blue (DMC 3325)
- ■ Bright yellow (DMC 726)

- Faded yellow (DMC 745)
- ▬ Dark gray (DMC 414)
- ▬ Slate blue (DMC 3885)
- ▬ Very light gray (DMC 762)
- ▬ Red (DMC 321)

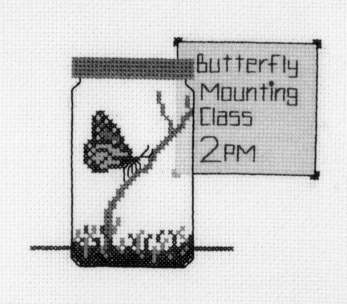

Butterfly
Mounting
Class
2 PM

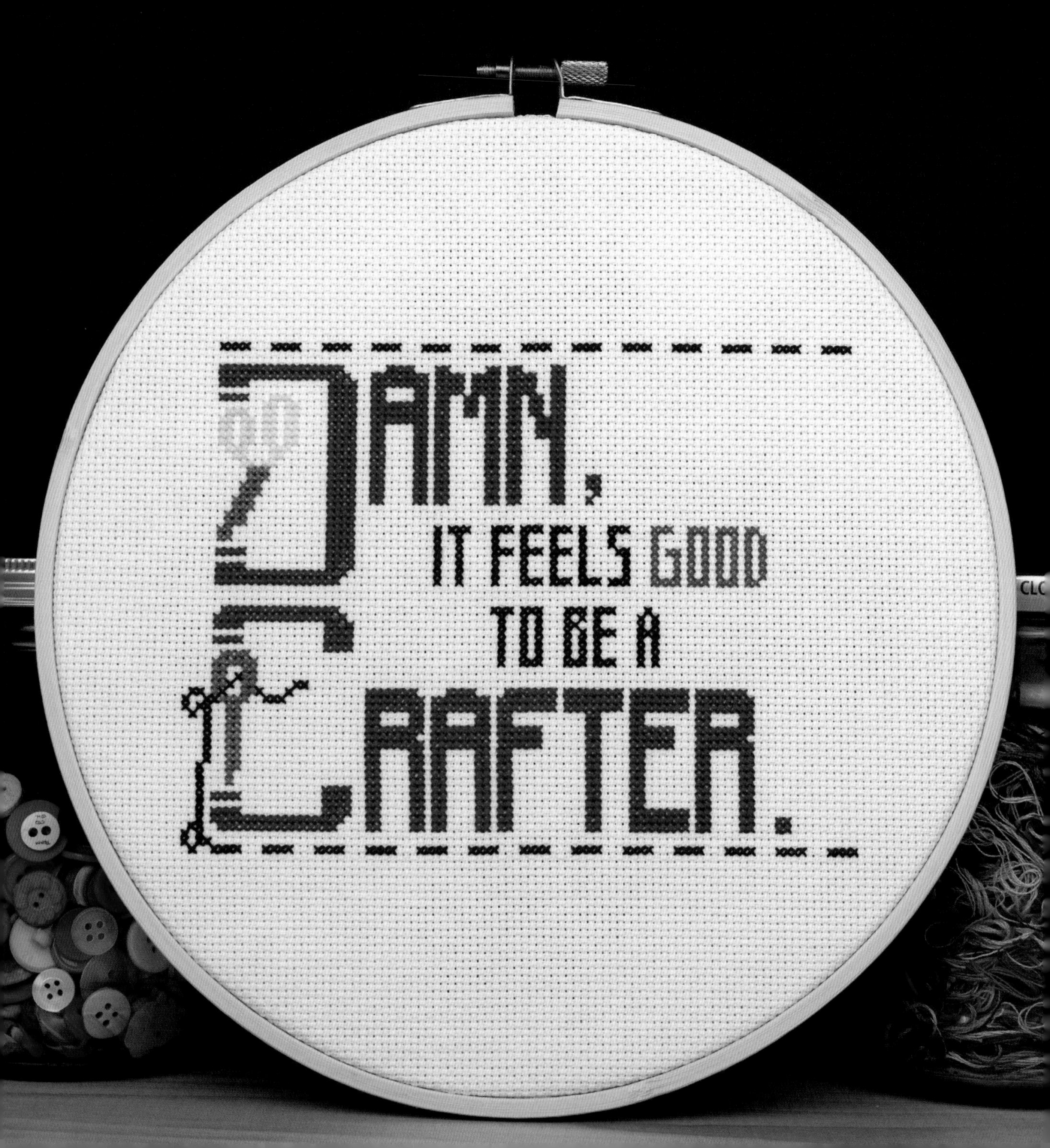
DAMN,
IT FEELS GOOD
TO BE A
CRAFTER.

- ■ Teal blue (DMC 3847)
- ■ Blue (DMC 796)
- ■ Dark pink (DMC 3804)
- ■ Dark gray (DMC 414)
- ▨ Bright yellow (DMC 726)

5. TALK NERDY TO ME

List of Patterns

- No Prince Necessary
- Evil Genius
- Talk Nerdy to Me
- Morning Cup of Chemistry
- Girls in Glasses
- Grammar Police
- Squad Goals
- Smart Is the New Sexy
- Robot Love
- Written in the Stars

Does your idea of the perfect date begin at the planetarium and end with a little light cosplay? Well, you've come to the right place! Welcome to the Talk Nerdy to Me pattern section. We have books and tea.

No Prince Necessary

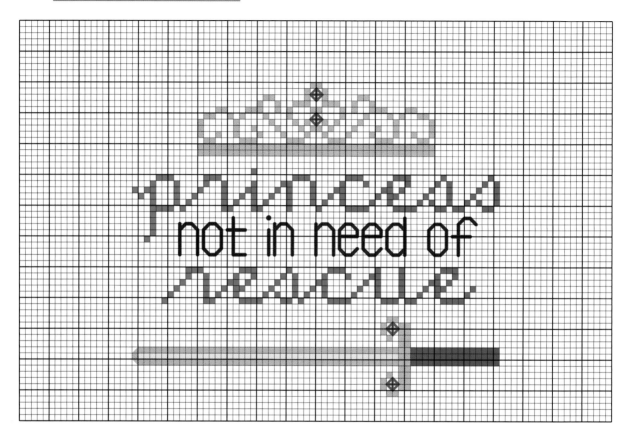

- ■ Slate blue (DMC 3885)
- ▦ Dark gray or metallic silver (DMC 414/E168)
- ▢ Very light gray (DMC 762)
- ■ Dark pink (DMC 3804)
- ▬ Black (DMC 310)
- ▬ Slate blue (DMC 3885)
- ● Black (DMC 310)

Evil Genius

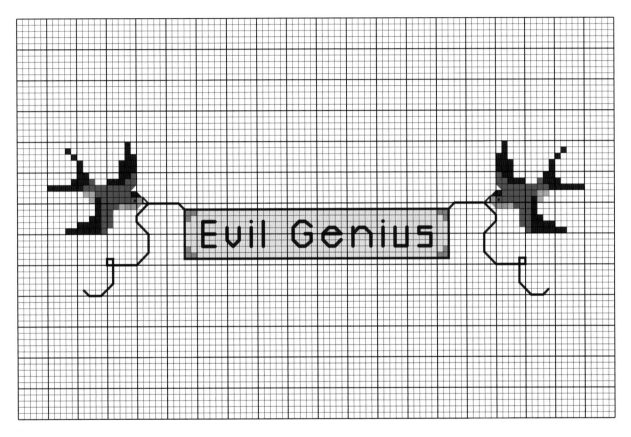

- ■ Blue (DMC 796)
- ■ Light blue (DMC 3843)
- ■ Salmon pink (DMC 3833)
- ■ Beige (DMC 644)
- ■ Pale violet (DMC 153)
- ■ Gold or metallic gold (DMC 680/E3852)
- ▬ Black (DMC 310)
- ▬ Blue (DMC 796)
- ● Black (DMC 310)

Talk Nerdy to Me

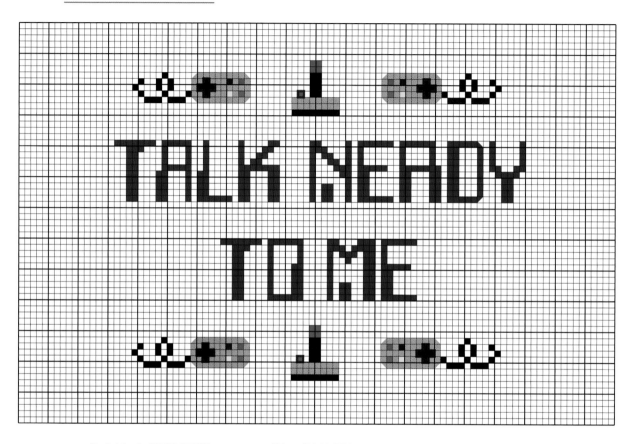

- ■ Soft black (DMC 3799)
- ■ Forest green (DMC 986)
- ■ Green (DMC 701)
- ■ Red (DMC 321)
- ■ Blue (DMC 796)
- □ Very light yellow (DMC 727)
- ■ Dark gray (DMC 414)
- ▬ Soft black (DMC 3799)
- ▬ Red (DMC 321)

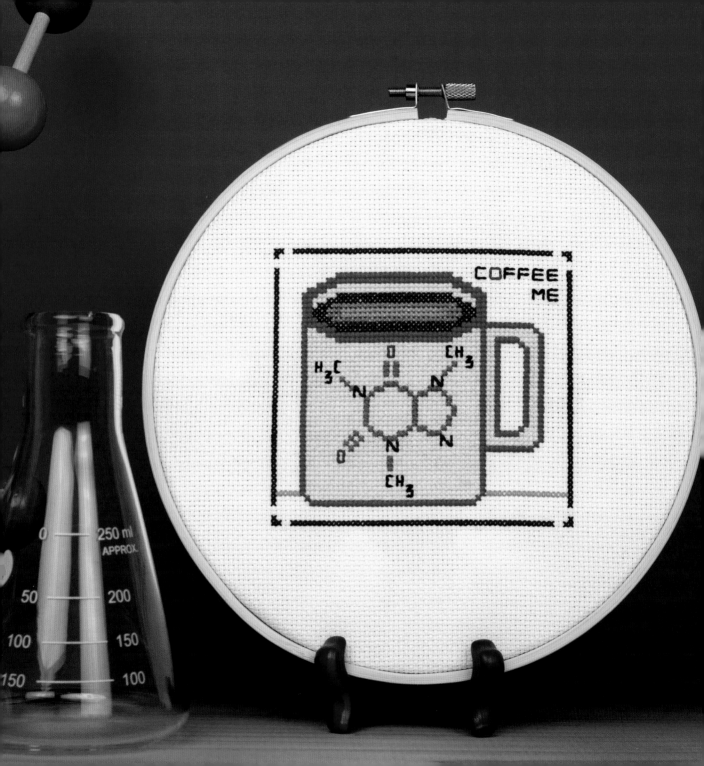

Morning Cup of Chemistry

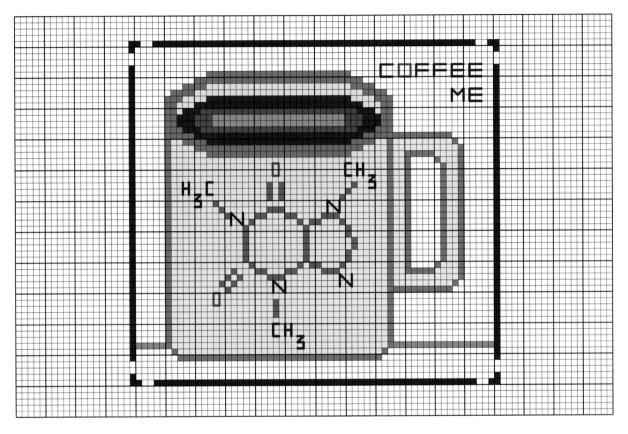

- ■ Light blue (DMC 3843)
- ■ Blue (DMC 796)
- Very light gray (DMC 762)
- ■ Green (DMC 701)
- ■ Brown (DMC 838)
- ■ Medium brown (DMC 840)
- ■ Tan (DMC 3045)
- ■ Orange (DMC 740)
- ▬ Red (DMC 321)
- ▬ Black (DMC 310)
- ▬ Blue (DMC 796)

Girls in Glasses

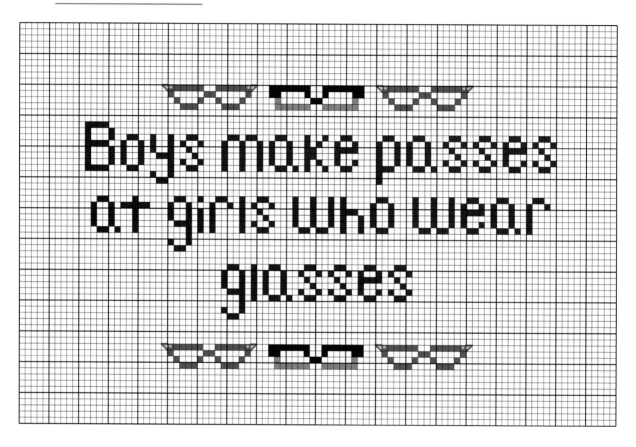

- ■ Black (DMC 310)
- ■ Blue (DMC 796)
- ■ Red (DMC 321)
- ■ Dark gray (DMC 414)
- ▬ Red (DMC 321)
- ● Metallic silver (DMC E168)

Grammar Police

- ■ Black (DMC 310)
- ■ Blue (DMC 796)
- ■ Light blue (DMC 3843)
- ■ Brick red (DMC 815)
- ■ Salmon pink (DMC 3833)
- ■ Grass green (DMC 989)

- ■ Medium purple (DMC 340)
- ■ Beige (DMC 644)
- ▨ Very light gray (DMC 762)
- ■ Gold or metallic gold (DMC 680/E3852)
- ▨ Faded yellow (DMC 745)
- ☐ White (DMC B5200)

- ▬ Black (DMC 310)
- ▬ Brick red (DMC 815)
- ▬ Salmon pink (DMC 3833)
- ▬ Light blue (DMC 3843)

- ■ Charcoal gray (DMC 413)
- ■ Light baby blue (DMC 3325)
- ■ Grass green (DMC 989)
- ■ Salmon pink (DMC 3833)
- ■ Medium purple (DMC 340)
- ▬ Charcoal gray (DMC 413)
- ▬ Slate blue (DMC 3885)
- ▬ Dark forest green (DMC 699)
- ▬ Brick red (DMC 815)
- ▬ Dark violet (DMC 3887)
- ● Slate blue (DMC 3885)

SQUAD GOALS.

BRONTË AUSTEN DICKINSON PLATH

Smart Is the New Sexy

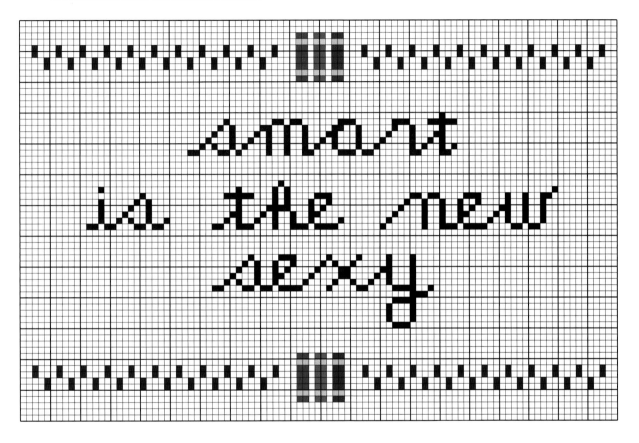

- ■ Black (DMC 310)
- ■ Blue (DMC 796)
- ▨ Light gray (DMC 415)
- ■ Ruby red (DMC 816)
- ■ Light blue (DMC 3843)
- ■ Forest green (DMC 986)
- ▨ Metallic copper or dark yellow (DMC E301/972)

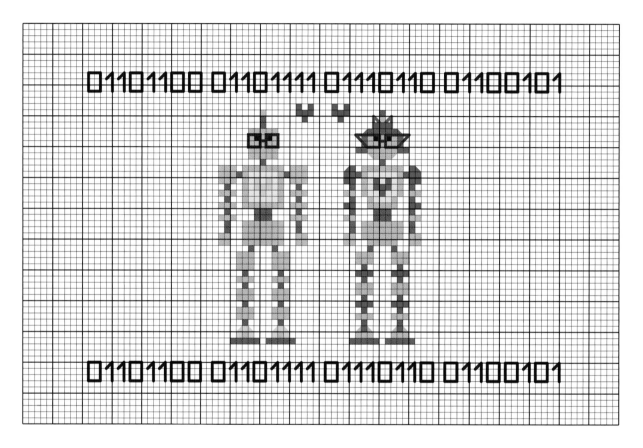

01101100 01101111 01110110 01100101

01101100 01101111 01110110 01100101

- ■ Blue (DMC 796)
- ■ Charcoal gray (DMC 413)
- ■ Light gray (DMC 415)
- Very light gray (DMC 762)

- ■ Green (DMC 701)
- ■ Bright yellow (DMC 726)
- ■ Red (DMC 321)
- ➖ Dark purple (DMC 333)

- ➖ Black (DMC 310)
- ➖ Green (DMC 701)
- ➖ Blue (DMC 796)

Written in the Stars

- ■ Soft black (DMC 3799)
- ■ Dark gray (DMC 414)
- ■ Very light gray (DMC 762)
- ■ Red (DMC 321)
- ■ Baby blue (DMC 827)
- ■ Very light yellow (DMC 727)
- ▬ Dark gray* (DMC 414)

*Use 1 strand (1 ply) of embroidery floss for constellation lines

6. ALPHABETS

List of Patterns

- ˣ Sans-Serif Alphabet
- ˣ Cursive Alphabet
- ˣ Line Alphabet

Because sometimes inside jokes and obscure *Firefly* references are just out there in the world, begging to be stitched, I've included three full alphabet patterns. Now, no opportunity for cross-stitched delight ever need be ignored.

Aa Bb Cc Dd Ee
Ff Gg Hh Ii Jj
Kk Ll Mm Nn Oo
Pp Qq Rr Ss Tt
Uu Uu Ww Xx Yy
Zz @1234567
8 9 ! ?

Cursive Alphabet

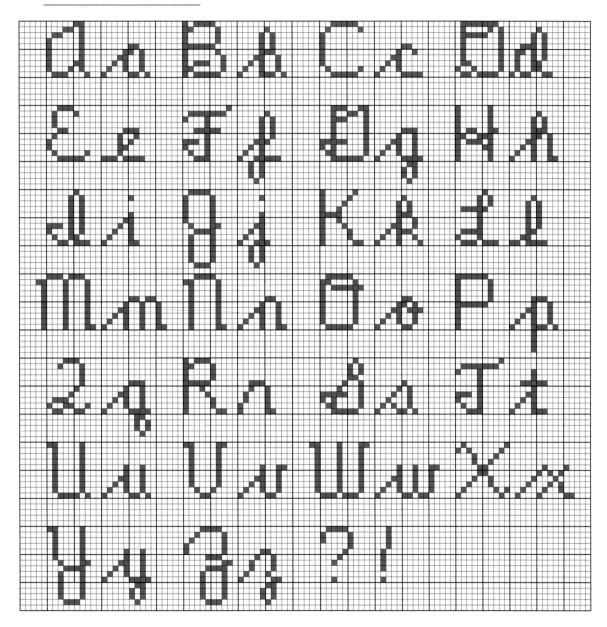

Line Alphabet

Aa Bb Cc Dd Ee Ff Gg

Hh Ii Jj Kk Ll Mm Nn

Oo Pp Qq Rr Ss Tt Uu

Uu Ww Xx Yy Zz

0123456789?!

7. FINISHING AND FRAMING

Finishing your work—cleaning, pressing, and preparing your piece for display—is the final step in any cross-stitch project, and it ensures that your stitches will look their very best for years to come.

Cleaning and Pressing

Once you're done stitching a new piece, or whenever a project stitched with washable fabric and floss starts to look dingy or dirty, give it a quick bath!

To wash a piece of cross-stitch, fill a clean sink or large bowl with cool water and add a small amount of a very mild laundry soap. (I usually use Soak laundry soap or Woolite.) Hand-wash your item, taking care not to rub or twist it. Unless you are absolutely certain that the dye in your floss is colorfast, do not submerge your projects for any longer than it takes to clean them, as dyes in floss can run and ruin your project. Rinse thoroughly with cool water, then gently roll the project up in a clean, light-colored towel and blot out as much water as possible. (Use two towels if necessary—the drier you can get your project, the less likely it is that the dyes in your floss will run!) Once it's blotted thoroughly, lay the piece flat to dry, gently squaring the fabric if needed so your design isn't distorted. *Never wring your projects out.*

When your project has dried completely, place a towel on your ironing board, then lay your stitching facedown, so the front is resting against the towel. (The towel will keep your stitching from getting crushed flat.) Place a pressing cloth or a clean piece of cotton fabric over your project to prevent scorch marks—your stitching should be sandwiched between the towel and the pressing cloth—then press your project gently using an iron with the steam setting turned on.

Framing and Displaying

There are many ways to display finished needlework, but two of the most common are framing or displaying in an embroidery hoop. Below, you'll find easy DIY methods for each.

Framing

Purchase an acid-free foam core board, then cut it to the size and shape that you'll need to fit inside your frame. Once the board is cut, center your project on top of it, then fold the excess fabric around the edges to the back of the board. Your centered design should lie smooth and taut across the board, with no bulges or wrinkles. If needed, you can use straight pins to hold your centered stitching in place temporarily.

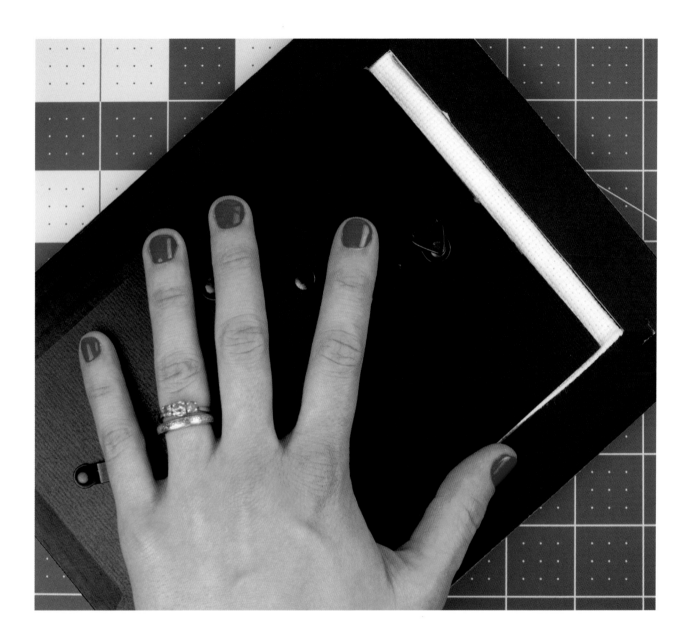

When you're happy with your project's placement, permanently secure the folded-back fabric to the board with archival mounting tape. Or, if you'd rather not make a permanent commitment, you can also hold the fabric in place using rust-free straight pins instead, angling them so they stick into the foam core board but don't poke through to the front of your project.

Place the mounted project inside the frame* then secure the frame's backing in place to finish.

Displaying in an Embroidery Hoop

Position your washed and pressed item in the embroidery hoop per usual, taking care to center the embroidery hoop's screw at the top of your work. Tighten the screw to secure the hoop, using a screwdriver if necessary. Once you're happy with the position of your project within the hoop, trim the fabric, leaving 1½–2 inches of extra fabric around the outside edge of the hoop.

IF YOUR HOOP IS WOODEN: On the back of your project, use an iron to carefully fold and press the fabric around the edges in toward the center of the hoop.

---

*Don't forget to remove the glass from the frame—admirers will want to see the stitch details!

IF YOUR HOOP IS PLASTIC OR A MATERIAL THAT CAN BE DAMAGED BY HEAT:
Facing the back of your project, sew a running stitch* around the edge of
the extra fabric, then bring the ends together to fold and gather the fabric
in toward the center on the back of your hoop. Tie the ends of the thread
together to secure (see illustration on page 108).

To prevent fraying around the fabric edges, and to ensure that the back
of your finished project lies flat, you can cover the back of your embroidery
hoop with a piece of felt or fabric, then whipstitch** it in place.

*As shown in the photo above, a running stitch is a simple line of evenly spaced stitches made by running the needle up and down through the fabric.

**As shown on page 109, whipstitching is a very simple way of neatly joining two pieces of fabric with evenly spaced stitches that encircle a seam. It's made by passing the needle from top to bottom through the two layers of fabric, gently pulling the thread taut, then reinserting the needle from top to bottom to start the next stitch, leaving a small, consistent amount of space between the current stitch and the previous stitch. As you continue whipstitching, you'll sew all the way around the edge of your project in a nearly circular spiral motion.

- -

Note: If you're planning to cover the back of your project, you can trace the inner ring of your embroidery hoop to create a pattern. If you're using fabric instead of felt, you'll also want to add at least a ¼-inch seam allowance to the pattern. Then, when you sew the fabric to the back of your project, the seam allowance should be turned under as you stitch to hide the raw edge of the fabric.

- -

Of course, if you'd like your finished projects to have heirloom-quality looks and longevity, but you don't have the time or the skills to DIY, you can always ask your local needlework or sewing shop to recommend a professional finisher for expert mounting and framing.

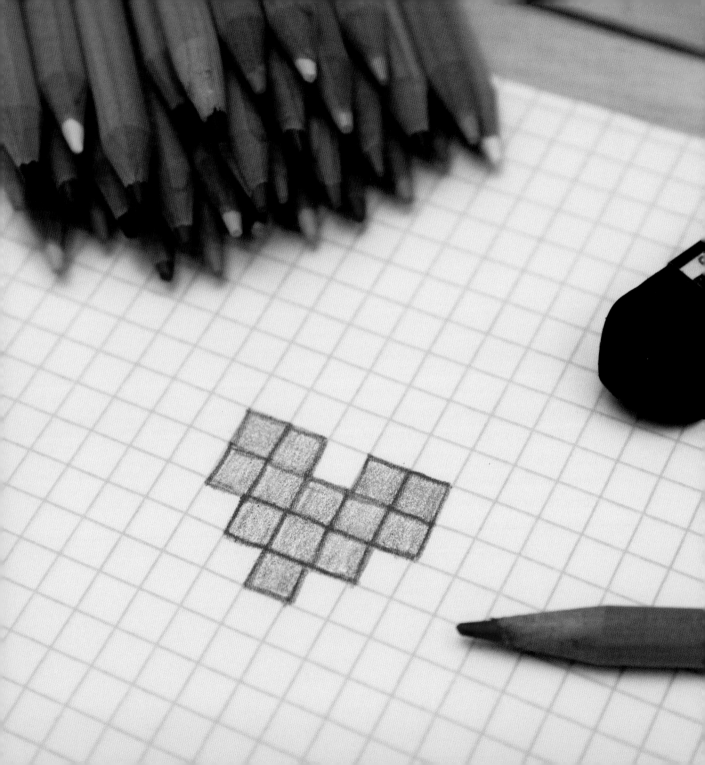

8. DESIGN YOUR OWN CUSTOM PATTERN

Now that you've stitched a few projects and feel confident that you know your way around an embroidery hoop and a skein of floss, you can use those stitching skills to make custom cross-stitch patterns of your own!

No design experience? No problem! While you certainly can use design software to make patterns, it's definitely not a requirement. Here's an easy, beginner-friendly method for charting the cross-stitch project of your dreams by hand.

Gather Your Supplies

To design your own cross-stitch patterns you'll need a few simple tools: graph paper, a pencil, a set of colored pencils, an eraser, and a ruler. And, if you're planning to design anything large or complicated, it's probably also a good idea to have a craft knife and roll of scotch tape on hand.

A note about graph paper: Keep in mind that if your graph paper doesn't have the same number of squares per inch as your cross-stitch fabric, your design will turn out either larger or smaller than your pattern chart when stitched.

If you want to make sure that your graph paper square size matches your fabric square size, either you can scour your local office supply store, or you can find free, printable graph paper templates for 14- and 28-count fabric on my website at www.redhandledscissors.com/graph-paper.

Find Your Inspiration

Before you get started, decide what you want to stitch. A phrase? A flower? Your cat?

Use the alphabets or other design elements in this book as a starting point, or just make it up as you go!

Sketch Out Your Idea (Or Just Wing It)

If you're planning a complex project, start by lightly sketching the general design and spacing on your graph paper. This will help you get the size and position of your designs just right.

Draw a Box

If you'd like your design to be a certain size, use your ruler and a pencil to draw a border box on your graph paper, then arrange your designs inside.

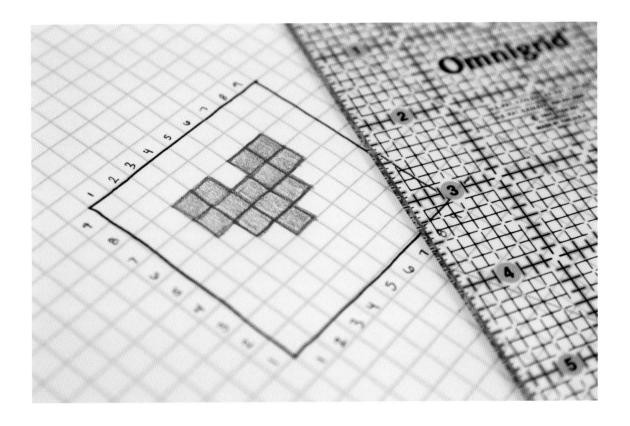

Number Your Grid

Number your grid so you don't lose your place while designing. I like to number all four sides of my grid, but you can stick to just the bottom and one side if that works best for you.

You may also want to mark the middle of your graph paper to help ensure that your designs are centered and balanced.

Start Coloring

Use colored pencils to build your designs by filling in the squares on the graph paper. Just like in the patterns in this book, one square on the graph paper will represent one cross-stitch.

Where should you start? There's no one right way to design a pattern, so take your personal preferences into account. Much the same as actually cross-stitching, some people might find it easier to work out from the center of the graph paper, while others might prefer to start at the top and go from there.

Fix Mistakes or Move Designs

If you screw up while you're working and an eraser just won't cut it—or if you decide you want to move design elements around to see what looks best—use a craft knife to carefully cut out the shape along the lines on the graph paper, then use scotch tape to attach the shape to a new sheet.